Living Free
A Guide to Forgiveness
and Restoration

*This book through the blood of Jesus and the word of God
can help to purge you of unforgiveness and the sins of your past,
which will put you in right standing with God.*

WINSOME CHERRY WILLIAMS

Six Hearts
publishing

LIVING FREE
A Guide to Forgiveness and Restoration

Cover design, Joel Ramjohn
Text pages design, Huntley Burgher
Author's photograph back cover: Thru Jen's Eyes

Published by Six Hearts Publishing
Davie, Florida 33328
www.sixheartspublishing.com

ISBN: 978-0-9845767-5-3
Library of Congress Control Number: 2011942895

Printed in the United States of America

DEDICATION

I am dedicating this book to my grandchildren, Genesis, Zion, Micah and Luke, as part of my legacy, I love you with all my heart!

I was only 9 when it all started...
How old were you?

PREFACE

Jealousy, pride, anger and bitterness can come from unforgive-ness, which wounds one's spirit and soul and I became guilty of them all. At the tender age of nine, I became jealous towards my older sister to whom I thought my mother was showing favoritism. Due to my jealousy, I became angry towards my mother and anger manifested in resentment and so my heart was the perfect place for pride.

I, however, have had a great relationship with my father and real-ized I had a special place in his heart, which made me even more prideful. The jealousy, pride and anger I had in my heart were not dealt with as a child and like most sins, it was swept under the rug. As a child, my life looked great on the outside but I was bitter on the inside even though I got all I thought I needed as a child grow-ing up on the island of Jamaica.

At age twenty four, I got married looking like a 'whole' person; but as life went on, jealousy met jealousy at another level which de-veloped into mistrust; mistrust became verbal and mental abuse, which aided in ending the marriage. Anger revisited, which be-came unforgiveness.

The heart of God permeated my heart and transformed my un-forgiving heart to one of forgiveness, love and compassion, thus inspiring this book 'Living Free.'

Unresolved past pain will cause present pain. I believe that one of the primary effects of unending strife and countless pain after a divorce occurs is due to the initial unwillingness to forgive. There-fore, I often use the phrase; ***"Hurt people, hurt other people."***

CONTENTS

ACKNOWLEDGEMENTS

The manifestation of this book is proof of God's faithfulness to me. The Lord Jesus has been waiting for me to completely trust Him regarding the publication of this book, and once I did, He made it possible. I thank God for His Holy Spirit, leading and guiding me into all truth.

Firstly, I would like to give honor to the Father, Son and Holy Spirit. I am eternally indebted to the incomparable grace of Almighty God for the abundant love and mercy that Jesus Christ has poured into my life through ministering and teaching on forgiveness and the wounded spirit.

I am grateful to my daughters for encouraging me to take a daily 'spiritual inventory' of my heart in the area of forgiveness. I must also thank God for Glenda Mitial, my first student, for sharing her life's journey with me. God allowed me to walk her through this teaching while He was teaching me love and forgiveness through His word. Thanks to my daughter Tanique, who helped with this book.

My spiritual parents: Mrs. Madge Silvera RN/MS, Dr. Albert Guthrie, and Dr. Mary Thompson. To my 'Pa' and 'Ma', Winston and Elaine Mullings for giving me all they could, to make me the person I am today. To some, I'm known as mom, Reverend Cherry, Winsome, Aunty Cherry, Mamma Cherry, Mommy Cherry, sis, and by my grandchildren- Genesis, Zion, Micah and Luke, whom I love dearly, I am known as Grandma Cherry and Pappa Cherry.

This project could not have been completed without the moral support provided through ongoing prayers, love, and even trials that have occurred throughout my life.

Psalm 119:67 & 71(NIV)... *"Before I was afflicted I went astray, but now I obey your word. It was good for me to be afflicted, so that I might learn your decrees."*

To my family and friends, biological and spiritual, thanks to you all. God has allowed me this privilege of serving within the context of intercession, deliverance and hospitality over the past years. It has been through difficulties, situations, challenges, experiences and testimonies that I have gained much of my own processing, helping me to better understand the power of Godís love, grace and forgiveness.

Revelation 12:11 (NIV)... *"They overcame him by the blood of the lamb and the word of their testimony, they did not love their lives so much as to shrink from death."*

ABOUT THE AUTHOR

Winsome Leona Williams, also known as 'Mama Cherry' was born in St. Andrew, Jamaica on December 18, 1954 to parents, Winston and Elaine Mullings, thus given the name Winsome from her father's name. The word 'winsome' means charming. God has graced her with a dynamic personality which she has used to reach out in evangelism, missionary work and hospitality. Leona is derived from the word 'lioness'. There is no doubt that God has blessed her with His supernatural strength so that she can be a blessing to others especially in the area of intercession. It has been prophesied and declared over her life that she carries a 'Deborah spirit'.

In order to be an effective leader, there are four basic qualities we must have and like Deborah, Winsome possesses these qualities:

• **Obedient to the voice of God:** After being a licensed cosmetologist for 30 years, God called Winsome to full-time ministry. She then released her profitable business, which she owned for over 10 years. The Bible says *'in all your ways acknowledge him and he shall direct your paths'* (Proverbs 3:6 KJV). For Winsome, being obedient to the Holy Spirit is non-negotiable.

• **Initiative to implement:** When Winsome's daughter, Tanique told her about the forgiveness training she attended during her discipleship training at Youth with a Mission (DTS), the Holy Spirit led her to share with her mother because she knew her mother was carrying around unforgiveness towards her (Tanique's) father. God broke down the walls of unforgiveness in Winsome's life through repentance and restitution and later called her to teach on forgiveness. After receiving her training through the Holy Spirit, she took the initiative and launched her ministry 'In His Will Ministries of South Florida'. She has ministered in Haiti, Santo Domingo, Jamaica, Israel, South East Asia and various states in the US.

• **Supportive of leadership:** Winsome was appointed as the Youth Pastor of Open Bible Community Church (OBCC) in 2004. Today, she remains a Pastoral Ministry Team member at the church and carries more of a supportive role in the lives of youth while walking out God's call on her life. In her workshops, she joins forces with other leaders so that together they can reach a broader audience.

Her objectives are to reach people for the Lord and see lives changed through forgiveness and restoration.

• **Audacity to trust God:** Everyday for her is a 'faith walk'. She does not give thought of what she will eat or what she will drink, because she knows that God will meet her needs according to His riches in Glory, therefore she gives and expects nothing in return. When you grace her house with your presence, you can feel the love of God 'bursting through its walls'. A Culinary artist by nature, she feeds her guests with food that is 'fit for a king' as she is inspired by the Holy Spirit. There is no lack in her life, spiritually or physically because she trusts the Lord with all her heart. She is a 'Ruth' to many of her sisters and a 'Naomi' to others, but to all of Gods people she is a mighty woman of God who is charged by Jesus and is committed to serve.

Nina Hart,
Author/speaker

FOREWORD

I am so excited about **'Living Free'**. Rev. Winsome Williams has been teaching on the godly principles of forgiveness through the love of God. Through spiritual insight, God has instructed Rev. Williams to teach His people to forgive and to have an agape love for one another. She desires to see the body of Christ completely healed from the spirit of unforgiveness and to receive His gift of freedom through forgiveness.

I have known Rev. Williams (Mommy Cherry) for 14 years and have watched her mentor others to walk in love and to live a life of obedience by listening to the voice of God for instructions concerning His work through their lives. She is also the founder/president of 'In His Will Ministries' which has hosted seminars, workshops, and prophetic teachings along with individual 'coaching' sessions. These sessions have brought about life changing experiences globally. Numerous testimonies have come forth to share how these various sessions have taught individuals as well as couples to live in forgiveness.

She is a mother of two daughters, along with two wonderful sons-in-law, four adorable grandchildren and has birthed many spiritual children, including myself. This woman of God continues to be an example of what agape love is and her lifestyle exemplifies her calling to teach on forgiveness by walking in God's love. Her focus is to emphasize how important it is for the body of Christ to embrace the power of forgiveness and to walk in the fullness of God's agape love.

Living Free will instruct you on how to walk in freedom, healing, and love! This book will not only challenge, but teach you how to live a life of love through forgiveness.

John 8:36–**"If the Son therefore shall make you free, ye shall be free indeed."**

Through her teachings, I not only received the gift of forgiveness, but I also am now able to give this gift to others. I was lost in a desolate place that consumed and crippled my emotions to feel anything but revenge toward my offender. How I longed to be free from this imprisonment that tormented me for years, when the Lord in His sovereign love, sent this woman of God to show me love and how to love others beyond my past pain. This freedom through forgiveness brought about a new way of life that I now desire to see others experience.

Minister Glenda Mitial,
Go Ye Community Church of God

Locust

Caterpillar

Cankerworm

"And I will restore to you the years that the locust hath eaten, the cankerworm and the caterpillar, and the palmerworm, my great army which I sent among you"
Joel 2:25-28

Jealousy.
Saul was jealous of David.
1 Sam. 24:17

Palmerworm

Anger
Eccl. 7:9

CONSECRATION PRAYER

Lord Jesus, I come as Your daughter/son, seeking to draw closer to You in my heart. Therefore, Lord, I am asking for Your Holy Spirit to bring conviction to my heart and reveal any area which needs cleansing. Blessed Holy Spirit, I repent for not always being open to Your Holy Spirit's nudging and leading in my life and for listening to the voice of the enemy. I want to respond only to the sound of your still small voice as you alert me. I am determined to no longer be a tool for the enemy to use, but will be a channel for the Holy Spirit to flow in and through.

Wash me clean from my guilt, and purify me from my sins. Create in me a clean heart, O God; and renew a right spirit within me. I am a warrior for the Kingdom of God and will remain faithful and obedient to do all that you ask of me. Empower me Lord, to be all that I can be through the Blood of Jesus. I will position myself as a woman/man of God, so that I can distinguish the 'noise' of distraction from Your voice. Anoint me with integrity, wisdom and joy needed to fulfill my destiny. Help me to see that you have already impregnated me with a vision and a calling to please you, Lord. Help me to walk in the fullness of Your original plan for my life. And I ask for the joy of the Lord to be my strength as I continue in faith by the power of the blood of Jesus.

In Jesus Mighty name! Amen!

Take a moment and think about your life and your future. Is there anything else you want to say to the Lord or repent of as you are asking God to consecrate you?

_____

_____

_____

_____

_____

_____

_____

_____

_____

_____

_____

_____

_____

_____

_____

_____

_____

_____

_____

_____

_____

_____

_____

UNDERSTANDING GOD'S HEART TOWARDS YOU
(The Father Heart of God)

God is:

- El Elohim–all powerful God

- El Roi–the God who sees me

- El Shaddai–the all sufficient God

- Jehovah Jireh–the Lord who provides

- Jehovah Shammah–the Lord who is present (with us in our pain)

- Jehovah Rohi–our Shepherd (God allows painful circumstances to help correct and heal us)

- Jehovah Shalom- our perfect comforter, the Lord of peace

- Jehovah Nissi– the Lord our banner. His banner over us is love.

- Trustworthy

- Jealous

- All knowing

- One who values us

- A good teacher

- He is our kinsman redeemer

- A good father (Psalm 68:5, 103:13)–earthly fathers can sometimes taint our view of the word 'father' and therefore taint our view of God as a Father. The ultimate role of a father is to have a relationship with his children.

God is not:

- One who abandons or abuses his children

- An unjust disciplinarian even though he DOES discipline us in love.

- Inconsistent with His love

However, God loves us too much to leave us in the state we are in (wounded and unforgiving).

What is the Source of Your Pain?

_____
_____
_____
_____
_____
_____
_____
_____
_____
_____
_____
_____
_____
_____
_____
_____
_____
_____
_____
_____
_____
_____

A WOUNDED SPIRIT

The wounded spirit is a person's spirit which has been hurt by a circumstance or series of circumstances that have occurred over the course of their life. This pain or wound has 'paralyzed' them from reaching their complete freedom in God. It is usually a dark area in the heart where the pain that has been afflicted upon the individual remains hidden, yet often will affect their life and relationships negatively.

There are wounds of the body and wounds of the spirit. The physical wound can usually be healed with good medical care, but only God can heal the wounds of the spirit. There is no hospital or physician, medical doctor or holistic doctor who can heal the wounds of the spirit. No medical personnel, whether it is a doctor or a nurse, can help the inner pain and grief caused by a wounded spirit. These are the wounds the hymn writer sings about in the song "Take it to the Lord in Prayer."

Many of us who have been wounded spiritually become unforgiving, angry, fearful, and bitter. It often affects our lives and the lives of others. This allows the spirit of unforgiveness to take hold of us and control that area of our lives. This wounded spirit could take root in the lives of the descendants of the ones who have been hurt thus creating a generational curse of unforgiveness, bitterness, fear and anger.

Ezekiel 18:2 KJV makes reference to the Proverbs that states that ***"the fathers have eaten sour grapes, and the children's teeth are set on edge."*** This is a curse that is passed down from father to son, and generations thereafter.

The Bible also speaks of "wounded spirits" in Proverbs 18:14 ***"The spirit of a man will sustain his infirmity but a wounded spirit who can bear?"***

God says you cannot handle a wounded spirit. We cannot bear a wounded and broken spirit. We know of people in our lives that are trying to bear this, but truly are not meant to. If your spirit is not whole, or if you are broken, crippled and walking wounded, you're not whole. The wound will manifest through your emotions, anger, bitterness, bad attitude and much more which tends to give off an awful stench, in some cases.

WAYS OUR SPIRIT CAN BE WOUNDED
Spoken Words

Our words can bruise, hurt, fracture, and injure our spirit.

Colossians 3:21 says *"Fathers, do not provoke your children lest they become discouraged."*

The word provoke means to initiate or discourage (children) by harsh yelling or nagging and degrading their efforts. Such provocation wounds their spirit and can allow them to become unforgiving, fearful, angry, timid and discouraged. This may cause a child or an adult to fail at life-efforts or have low self esteem.

With a lack of knowledge, we may speak words to loved ones that affect them negatively, but God is a Father who forgives. It is important when we recognize that we have done this to ask God and the person you offended to forgive you.

"A wholesome tongue is a tree of life: but perverseness therein is a breach in the spirit" Proverbs 15:4

Words are a carrier of the Spirit. (Matthew 12:35-37)

God hates a slandering tongue; a tongue that spreads mischief (gossip). The Lord is displeased when we spread rumors or gossip. Miriam and Aaron gossiped about Moses. Dealing with forgiveness is not necessarily covering or keeping our mouths shut about the hurt that has been afflicted upon us, but making it into gossip will only enlarge the circle of your repentance and the circle of your forgiveness. Each person you have pulled into the circle of your gossip in unforgiveness will need to be approached and asked for their forgiveness for pulling them into your circle of sin.

Our circle of sin equals our circle of repentance.

There are certain evil or wicked people who we need to warn others about so that they won't be deceived by them. We need to warn our children about people who could damage or hurt them in your absence.

However, a bitter person may spread a story, whether it is true or false, against God's people. It is dangerous to the soul of the one who does this as well as to the victim, as it could harm the body of Christ.

"The words of a talebearer are as wounds, and they go down into the innermost parts of the bell". (Proverbs 18:8 NKJV)

The point is that we may be wounded by words that were spoken over us or we may have hurt others as a result of being wounded in our lives.

Never allow yourself to come under the curse of unforgiveness. But if you have, there is still hope in Christ to set you free from it. The Lord was cruelly wounded by those who lied on Him and accused Him of things He didn't say or do. But He forgave them because He did not want the spirit of unforgiveness to cleave to Him or His children of faith, which includes you and me. Jesus is the only one who can and will help us to forgive those who have wounded our spirit. Wounds will heal if we allow forgiveness in our hearts and lives.

Ask God, "Has anyone wounded my spirit through their spoken words? How?"

Emotion Based Problems

"A merry heart doeth good like a medicine; but a broken Spirit drieth the bones." Proverbs 17:22

Emotion based problems can produce physical and spiritual symptoms. It has been shown that in some cases, arthritis can be acquired as a result of an emotion based problem or wound. Why does this occur? Because God said that we cannot bear a wounded spirit, and therefore the wound manifests itself into a physical form. Unforgiveness can contaminate your blood, proven by medical doctors.

Ask God, "Has anyone wounded my spirit through my emotions? How?"

_____

_____

_____

_____

_____

_____

_____

_____

_____

_____

_____

_____

_____

_____

_____

_____

_____

_____

_____

_____

_____

_____

_____

_____

_____

_____

_____

_____

_____

Spirit of Sorrow

Proverbs 15:13–*"A merry heart maketh a cheerful countenance; but by sorrow of heart the spirit is broken."*

In the case of the loss of a loved one or in a divorce or separation, one can be left with feelings of abandonment and rejection.

Jesus carried our sorrows; He was wounded for our transgressions so that He can heal us. Jesus' spirit was wounded but he never functioned out of the wound. He himself took our infirmities and bore our sickness. Matthew 8:17.

Jesus wants to heal every hurt and every wound but we must ask Him! 1 Peter 2:24 NIV states that *"by His wounds you have been healed."*

Ask yourself "Has there been any sorrowful situation in my life that has wounded my spirit?" (Death of a loved one, divorce, disappointment in a person).

_____

_____

_____

_____

_____

_____

_____

_____

_____

_____

_____

_____

_____

_____

_____

_____

_____

_____

_____

_____

_____

_____

_____

_____

_____

Sexual Sins

Proverbs 6:32–**"But whoso committeth adultery with a woman lacketh understanding; he that doeth it destroyeth his own soul."**

Sexual activity during a dating relationship or engagement can invite a wounded spirit into the marriage. When the novelty of the 'secret lustful relationship' has ended and commitment and responsibility become a reality within the bonds of marriage, often the novelty of 'stealing love' ends. One party's sexual expectation may no longer seem as if it is being met and they may even seek another avenue to selfishly fulfill this unrealistic desire. This selfish mindset can then wound the marriage.

Sexual sins include lust, having multiple sexual partners, adultery and fornication. These sexual sins open the doors to other spirits. We should be careful of the way in which we expose our small children to parental nakedness.

Homosexuality, masturbation, and oral sex can be door openers that can lead to unforgiveness, fear and anger.

Sexual involvements affect our spiritual realities because during the act of sexual intercourse, the two people become one. Sex is not just physical; it is spiritual as we are spiritual beings, living souls, and a living spirit.

The devil isn't mainly after our flesh; he is after our souls.

Sex outside of marriage, whether in fornication or adultery can wound your spirit. This is not God's plan for your life. Multiple sex-partners will bring multiple spirits thus creating a domino effect, which will wound you.

Masturbation is a topic that the church does not like to talk about. It is a form of sexual activity as well as oral sex, which can also wound your spirit. (This is an animalistic behavior, smelling and tasting before mating). If God gives you specific conviction on these or other sexually related issues, you must be willing to deal with them immediately so that it's power may be broken. I felt that the Lord clearly revealed to me that masturbation brings some satisfaction but has the potential to lead to other sins, which may include homosexuality.

Confession of sin needs to be specific for the purpose of deliverance. Be willing to be open to the Lord as he already is aware of our 'hidden sins'.

Ask "Have I been wounded through sexual relationship/s or through sexual abuse that occurred in my past?"

_____
_____
_____
_____
_____
_____
_____
_____
_____
_____
_____

"For God will bring every deed into judgment, including every hidden thing, whether it is good or evil". Ecclesiastes 12:14

Alcoholism

Alcoholism can be a wound in many families.

Who has woe? Who has sorrow? Who has strife? Who has complaints? Who has needless bruises? Who has bloodshot eyes? Those who linger over wine, who go to sample bowls of mixed wine. Do not gaze at wine when it is red, when it sparkles in the cup, when it goes down smoothly! In the end it bites like a snake and poisons like a viper. Your eyes will see strange sights and your mind imagine confusing things. You will be like one sleeping on the high seas, lying on top of the rigging. "They hit me," you will say, "but I'm not hurt! They beat me, but I don't feel it! When will I wake up so I can find another drink?" Proverbs 23:29-35

In the case of alcoholism, at times it may accompany physical and/ or mental abuse. Excessive drinking of alcohol can affect relationships negatively as the person may not be in full control of their actions at the moment. Alcoholism can also weaken a person's ability to withstand temptation and allow them to be more susceptible to acting out in ways they may not normally do if they were sober.

**Ask "Have I been wounded by alcohol, whether through
my own abuse of it, or someone else inflicting it on
my life?"**

_____
_____
_____
_____
_____
_____
_____
_____
_____
_____
_____
_____
_____
_____
_____
_____
_____
_____
_____
_____
_____
_____
_____
_____
_____
_____

False Prophets

"The prophets prophesy lies, the priests rule by their own authority, and my people love it this way. But what will you do in the end?" Jeremiah 5:31 NKJV

As children growing up, we tend to depend on our parents to be the models in our lives and to be the ones who bring the greatest encouragement about our potential. There have been many godly parents who have been great examples to their children. However, in other cases, parents have misused their authority to speak poisonous words instead of life giving words into their children. These words later become so ingrained in the child's life that they can begin to act out and live out the negative things spoken over them. Damaging words can include speaking about how ugly, fat and stupid the child is. Parents sometimes will declare that the child will never amount to anything. Even as an adult, the words often continue to haunt the individual in marriage and other relationships as well as their careers. It can bring about great levels of insecurity and worthlessness in the person's life. *"Death and life are in the power of the tongue."* Proverbs 18: 21; Deuteronomy 30: 19-20.

Ask "Have I been wounded by false prophets in my life? If so, how?"

_____

_____

_____

_____

_____

_____

_____

_____

_____

_____

_____

_____

_____

Finally, ask God if there are any other ways that your spirit has been wounded. Make a note of them.

_____

_____

_____

_____

_____

_____

_____

_____

_____

_____

UNFORGIVENESS

Unforgiveness is as if I'm drinking deadly poison and expecting the person that I'm holding in unforgiveness to die.

Don't allow the infection of unforgiveness to make you sick mentally, physically, spiritually and emotionally anymore. The sins of bitterness, unforgiveness, resentment, anger and rage are as poison in your bloodstream and can hinder your spiritual growth.

The Lord forgave **NOT** some, but all our iniquities and healed all our diseases and redeemed our lives from destruction and crowned us with loving kindness and tender mercies. *"He satisfies our mouth with good things so that our youth is renewed like the eagles."* Psalm 103 vs. 5 (paraphrase)

Before we discuss what forgiveness is, let's see what forgiveness is not. Do not allow anger or fear to become deep rooted bitterness inside of your life.

- Forgiveness is NOT approval. Jesus forgave the woman caught in adultery, but He didn't approve of her sin; instead He told her to *"go and sin no more."* (Mark 11:25)

- Forgiveness is NOT excusing the reason why we did what we did to make it easier for us to be forgiven.

- Forgiveness is NOT pardoning–a legal term meaning "to release from consequences;" but while you cannot impose your consequences on the offender, you cannot shield them from God's dealing or judgment.

- Forgiveness is NOT denying or keeping it a secret. Only when we fully acknowledge and come to terms with what was done to us can we truly forgive. David's story: 2 Samuel 12.

- Forgiveness is NOT forgetting. It is impossible to forget any significant event. We choose not to allow it to rule our thoughts.

  Example; I will forgive but I will not forget (trust)

- Forgiveness is NOT assumption that the person understands forgiveness.

- Forgiveness is NOT reconciliation; that requires two people to be in agreement. What if one of them won't agree?

- Forgiveness is NOT remaining a victim.

- Forgiveness is NOT using the word 'but', which is partial forgiveness and total disobedience.

- Forgiveness is NOT reasoning out the offence in an effort to desensitize yourself.

- Forgiveness is NOT rehashing what they did to you

- Forgiveness is NOT guilt. Don't allow someone's choice not to forgive you to cause you to walk with guilt. (e.g.) When parents separate or become divorced, children who manipulate with their words can keep a parent or both parents in a place of feeling a false sense of guilt.

- Forgiveness is NOT a decision to ignore your pain.

HEALING THE WOUNDED SPIRIT

There comes a time when God says "ENOUGH". You can either deal with your wounds or your wounds will deal with you. You have to face your wounds or you may have to revisit your wound because you have to pass through it in order to get over it. Hurt people tend to hurt others. Do you want to continue to hurt yourself and your loved ones or are you willing to start a new journey of healing and freedom?

Seek God for comfort concerning your wounded spirit so that you do not end up in a circle of unforgiveness in which you may not be ready to start forgiving. Don't allow your spirit to be defiled. The Father's heart's desire is to keep our spirits clean from infectious wounds.

How do you know if there is a wound in your spirit inflicted by someone's words? You ask God!

You can ask Him: "If there is a wound there, Holy Spirit, place your hand on it and heal me." You will remember the wound because it comes with a reminder of pain. It is important to set aside time with God so that you can hear His still small voice.

Ask God "Has anyone spoken a word into my life that has wounded my spirit?"

You may need to allow the Holy Spirit time to point out any wound(s) in your spirit. He knows and sees them before you ask Him. So why continue to live a wounded life when Jesus Himself was wounded on our behalf but did not live a wounded life. So, let go and let God. Watch your thoughts, they will become words; words become actions, actions become habits, habits become character, and character becomes your destiny.

Make a list of person(s) or events that might have wounded you through words spoken. e.g. having an abortion.

One word spoken by an authority figure can hold you in bondage all the days of your life until you come to God and say:

"Lord I forgive _____for what he/ she said, I release this charge against them now, please heal the wounds in my spirit." By Jesus' stripes and in your name Jesus I pray!

Forgiveness by itself will not completely heal a wounded spirit even though it is necessary to forgive. Forgiveness deals with making our heart right before God! You will need to go deeper with Jesus' stripes to get total healing as you walk in forgiveness.

Jesus said in John 6:63 that words are 'spirit and life'. Therefore you must begin to speak life over yourself, other people and situations.

Jesus never allowed His wound to become a part of His character. He became an offering to the Father and never a sacrifice to the wound. We should be a living sacrifice of praise to the Father and not a sacrifice to the wounds of our spirit.

The objective of healing the wounded spirit is not to dig up 'old bones' or old wounds. For you to be healed of a wounded spirit, you must revisit the root that caused the wound.

It is impossible to take anyone any further in the Lord than you are in Him. We must be ministers who are healed and whole and able to reproduce healed and whole ministers of the Gospel of Jesus Christ. The Father's heart is for us to live a complete life in His love through Jesus Christ.

The Bible speaks of "wounded spirits" in Isaiah 1:5-6;

Why should you be beaten anymore? Why do you persist in rebellion? Your whole head is injured, your whole heart afflicted. From the sole of your foot to the top of your head there is no soundness, only wounds and welts and open sores, not cleansed or bandaged or soothed with oil.

When the Lord spoke of Israel's wounds, he was not speaking of physical wounds but their wounds of sin. Wounds are inflicted when sin is present, so whether you sin or someone sins against you, a wound may be inflicted. As in the case of being stabbed, the one who is stabbed is the victim and also the wounded one. Jeremiah also speaks of Israel's wounds in Jeremiah 8:18-22

"O my Comforter in sorrow, my heart is faint within me. Listen to the cry of my people from a land far away: Is the LORD not in Zion? Is her King no longer there? Why have they provoked me to anger with their images, with their worthless foreign idols? The harvest is past, the summer has ended, and we are not saved. Since my people are crushed, I am crushed; I mourn, and horror grips me. Is there no balm in Gilead? Is there no physician there? Why then is there no healing for the wound of my people?"

The Lord had seen their sinful state and the wounds that occurred as a result of their sins and he asked the questions in vs. 22 *"Is there no balm in Gilead; is there no physician there?"*

Balm was a mixture of herbs applied to a wound in that time. Gilead was a fertile region South East of the Sea of Galilee where they would pick these herbs for the care of the wound(s). I have been to Israel and it is a fact that rosemary and many other healing herbs grow wild along the highway or main roads.

Jeremiah is, in essence, asking the question "is there no balm for his people's spiritual wounds?" Is there no balm in Gilead? That was their source of healing but we now have the Great Physician and His name is Jesus. Through Jesus' death on the cross, we can be healed and freed.

Isaiah 61:1 is quoted by Jesus in Luke 4:18, ***"The Spirit of the Lord is upon me, because he hath anointed me to preach the gospel to the poor; he hath sent me to heal the brokenhearted, to preach deliverance to the captives, and recovering of sight to the blind, to set at liberty them that are bruised."***

Jesus is our healing balm, the healer of our spiritual wounds. The heart of God our Father is to see us more like His original plan, which is made in His image and likeness–the likeness of Jesus.

In Isaiah 1:5-6, the moral and spiritual condition of Israel was transferred to the suffering servant. In Isaiah 53:4-5 ***"and by His stripes we are healed"*** but in Matthew 7:7-8 it says you have to ask God to heal you and you **shall** receive your healing!

"Ask, and it shall be given you, seek and ye shall find, knock and it shall be opened unto you: for everyone that asketh receiveth and he that seeketh findeth and to him that knocketh it shall be opened."

Be healed; be made whole from the wounded spirit by the power of the blood of Jesus Christ!

Receive and walk and live in your healing. Now that you have received healing, know that you may be wounded again. Remember to continue a lifestyle of forgiveness and ask Jesus to heal your wound as soon as it occurs.

Don't allow your wounds to color the pages of your life and then treat others the way you were treated. Jesus heals the broken hearted.

"He was wounded for our transgressions, He was bruised for our iniquity. The chastisement for our peace was upon Him and with His stripes we are healed." Isaiah 53:5

RESTORATION THROUGH FORGIVENESS

"And I will restore to you the years that the locust hath eaten, the cankerworms and the caterpillars and palmerworms, my great army which I sent among you." Joel 2:25

Restoration of our heart occurs when we make the decision and choice to forgive. God wants to restore us no matter what has happened in our past or who has wounded us. God, through Jesus Christ's work on the cross, wants to restore us totally. With God all things are possible.

"And so we know and rely on the love God has for us. God is love. Whoever lives in love lives in God, and God in him." 1 John 4:16

Real hurt comes from people. For example when all four parasites or worms attack any plant, working together one will destroy the leaf, the branch, the main stalk, and finally the root. At the end, the plant will totally be destroyed. It is in this same manner that we should watch our thoughts, words, actions, and character. The thoughts will become a word, the word will become an action, and the action will determine our character whether it be good or bad.

We all have a past of good and bad memories that affect our lives today. Some painful things might have happened to you as a child. Paul says in Philippians 3:13-14,

"Forgetting what lies behind... I press on towards the goal."

God is the only restorer of all hurts or wounds. God wants us to live a wholesome physical and spiritual life. For He said,

"I will restore health unto you and I will heal all your wounds," says the Lord–Jeremiah 30:17 NKJV.

No matter what has happened in your past, God's plan is to bring you to a place where the negative issues of the past will no longer affect your present or future life in Christ Jesus. God's Word promises to restore the fullness of our life.

FOUR DIMENSIONS OF FORGIVENESS:

- Forgiveness towards God

- Forgiveness towards self

- Forgiveness towards your offender

- Asking God to forgive and bless your offender

Forgiveness towards God

- Jonah held unto his anger towards God and his hatred to wards the people of Nineveh to the very end. The people repented and God forgave.

God has not sinned against us in any way but often we perceive that when tragic situations occur in our life, God is responsible because He allowed it to happen. We must release God through forgiveness in order to see his true heart for us. The truth is that when bad things happen to us, it hurts God's heart greatly. And therefore, he is not to be blamed for our past or present hurts.

"The nature and character of God is love, mercy, grace and forgiveness."

Forgiveness towards Self

- Many times, we are most unforgiving towards ourselves because of situations we have allowed ourselves to go through. We can find that sometimes the pain we experience from past wounds can be self inflicted. However, for giving ourselves is key to walking in freedom.

- Forgiveness can be an excellent weight loss program. When we go through depressing or hard issues, habits of excessive eating may be formed and thus lead into further depression that will often continue into a vicious cycle of unforgiveness.

- Forgiveness is not pretending you weren't hurt. It is recognizing that in order to be free, you must release those who have hurt you to God because, "Hurt people often Hurt other people."

  Look in the mirror and see how Jesus sees you... then choose to start forgiving yourself.

Forgiveness towards your offender

- Real forgiveness is a lifelong commitment and decision one makes by faith to obey God's Word and to live a life style pleasing to God in a higher dimension. You do this by not allowing someone else's actions, attitudes or character to determine your actions, attitude or character.

- Forgiveness is a gift given to us by God to give to those we think do not deserve it.

- Forgiveness will hurt, but it hurts even more to stay in bondage.

- Forgiveness kills the flesh; unforgiveness keeps us imprisoned.

- Forgiveness does not mean you will have to trust the person again. e.g. (stolen money or rape). Trust will come as change in that person's character is made evident. We can trust God because we know His character is love. (1 John 4:8-10). You know you have forgiven a person when you can see them as God sees them.

- Forgiveness is the glue that can repair broken relationships. *"God is love"* (1 John 4:8-10 and Revelation 12:11)

- Forgiveness allows God to move on your behalf and will free you from bondage to continue growing in the Lord. You will become the man or woman of God you have been called to be, in Jesus' name. Jesus called Judas friend when he was about to betray Him. Matthew 26 v 50 KJV

"This is how I want you to conduct yourself in these matters. If you enter your place of worship and, about to make an offering, you suddenly remember a grudge a friend has against you, abandon your offering, leave immediately, go to this friend and make things right. Then and only then, come back and work things out with God." Matthew 5 vs. 23-24   (The Message Bible)

"Father forgive them for they don't know what they are doing." Luke 23:34 (NLT)

"For if you forgive men when they sin against you, your heavenly father will also forgive you. But if you do not forgive men their sins, your heavenly father will not forgive your sins." Matthew 6:14 (KJV)

If you think having unforgiveness towards the living is hard, try having unforgiveness towards the dead. The grave cannot speak. This can be bondage at its fullest!

Asking God to forgive and bless your offender

*   Pray asking God to forgive them for the ways they have hurt you.

*   Bless them! After you have forgiven the individual, it is im portant to also pray a blessing over them.

Forgive me

This exercise can be used for self-forgiveness for the victim or the offender.

Look in the mirror and see how Jesus sees you...

I forgive myself for having unforgiveness in my heart...

Free me of doubt, anger, and bitterness.

"There is therefore now no condemnation to them which are in Christ Jesus." Romans 8:1

Father God,

- Forgive me for allowing _____ to put fear in my heart.

- Forgive me for allowing _____ to create bitterness in my heart.

- Forgive me for allowing _____ to create hatred in my heart.

- Forgive me for allowing _____ to hurt me.

- Forgive me for allowing _____ to have power over me

- Forgive me for allowing _____ to repeatedly manipulate me.

- Forgive me for allowing _____ to steal my innocence.

- Forgive me for allowing _____ to control my emotions.

- Forgive me for allowing _____ to intimidate me.

APPLYING FORGIVENESS

It is important to evaluate the condition of your heart to see if there is pain or wounds that you are nurturing. Allow the Holy Spirit to remind you of any offense that you have carried towards someone in your past or present who may have wounded you. You must be willing to set aside time alone in the presence of the Lord so that you are better able to discern and focus on His voice. As he speaks in that still small voice, make note of any names or events he may point out to you. When this happens, be willing to deal with it immediately. Once you have dealt with the most painful experiences, it will be easier to continue to deal with other smaller areas of unforgiveness in your heart. Once you are aware of those you need to forgive, make the choice to declare out loud that you have forgiven the offender/s. Finally, pray a prayer of blessing over your offender.

Make note of those who affected your life (positively (P) or negatively (N)). Place P/N next to their name.

_____

_____

_____

_____

_____

_____

_____

_____

_____

_____

_____

_____

_____

Take a minute to search your heart and see if you are carrying any unforgiveness towards God and take time to release Him through a prayer of repentance and forgiveness. Are you ready to stop blaming God for your pain?

You may say "Father I choose to release my... (anger, doubt, disbelief) towards you. I know that you are a loving Father who has always had my best interest at heart. Now that I know that your love for me is so great, I repent of my doubt and for believing that you abandoned me in my moments of hurt and despair."

* God

_____

_____

_____

_____

_____

_____

_____

_____

_____

_____

_____

Then ask God,

"Has anyone spoken a negative word into my life that has wounded my spirit or hurt me?" Has this person by their actions wounded me?

When forgiving your offender, it is important to state that you choose to forgive them instead of saying "Lord, help me to forgive" or "I want to forgive." We have all the tools we need to forgive. We only need to determine to make the choice to do it.

You may need to spend a little time on each one and give the Holy Spirit time to search for any wound(s). Make notes where applicable.

- **Mother**–e.g. spoken word while in the womb in regards to wanting you, and after you were born whether you should have been aborted or not. Passing through the womb with painful words.

  I choose to forgive my mother for...

  _____

  _____

  _____

  _____

  _____

  _____

  _____

  _____

  _____

  _____

  _____

  _____

  _____

  _____

  _____

  _____

- **Father**–e.g. when he was told that your mother was pregnant, he made inappropriate comments. (e.g. not ready to be a parent)

  I choose to forgive my father for...

  _____

  _____

  _____

  _____

  _____

  _____

  _____

  _____

  _____

- **Husband**- e.g. mental and physical/verbal abuse

  I choose to forgive my husband for...

  _____

  _____

  _____

  _____

  _____

  _____

  _____

  _____

  _____

- **Wife**–e.g. Comments regarding husband's leadership and character.

  I choose to forgive my wife for...

  _____

  _____

  _____

  _____

  _____

  _____

  _____

- **Pastor/Spiritual Leader**–e.g. one word spoken by an authority figure can empower you or wound you for life.

  I choose to forgive my pastor for...

  _____

  _____

  _____

  _____

  _____

  _____

  _____

  _____

- Notice, all of the above are Authority figures.

- **Self**

  - I choose to forgive myself for allowing_____
    to put fear in my heart.

  - I choose to forgive myself for allowing _____
    to create bitterness in my heart.

  - I choose to forgive myself for allowing _____
    to create hatred in my heart.

  - I choose to forgive myself for allowing _____
    to have power over me.

  - I choose to forgive myself for allowing _____
    to manipulate me over and over again.

  - I choose to forgive myself for allowing _____
    to control my emotions.

  - Lord, please forgive me!

I praise you because I am fearfully and wonderfully made; your works are wonderful, I know that full well. Psalm 139:14 NIV

For I know the thoughts that I think toward you, says the Lord, thoughts of peace and not of evil, to give you a future and a hope. Jeremiah 29:11 NKJV

- **Brother**–e.g. jealousy: favoritism from parents (Esau & Jacob)

  I choose to forgive my brother for...

  _____

  _____

  _____

  _____

  _____

  _____

  _____

- **Sister**–e.g. jealousy: favoritism from parents (Leah & Rebekah)

  I choose to forgive my sister for...

  _____

  _____

  _____

  _____

  _____

  _____

- **Children**–e.g. manipulation, neglect, bullying, fear

   I choose to forgive the children for...

   _____

   _____

   _____

   _____

   _____

   _____

- **Friends**–e.g. broken relationships; jealousy

   I choose to forgive my friends for...

   _____

   _____

   _____

   _____

   _____

   _____

- **Relatives**–e.g. prejudice, hatred, jealousy of achievement or success

   I choose to forgive my friends for...

   _____

   _____

   _____

   _____

   _____

- **Church**–e.g. leader's insecurity of who you are in Christ Jesus

  I choose to forgive the church leaders and congregants for...

  _____

  _____

  _____

  _____

- **Culture**–e.g. prejudice, superiority

  I choose to forgive my culture for...

  _____

  _____

  _____

  _____

"Therefore if any man be in Christ, he is a new creature: old things are passed away; behold all things are become new. And all things are of God, who hath reconciled us to himself by Jesus Christ, and hath given to us the ministry of reconciliation." 2 Corinthians 5:17-18 (KJV)

Questions to Answer

Are you willing to free yourself from bondage and allow the Lord, **NOT YOU,** to hold your offender accountable for their cruel actions towards you?

_____

_____

_____

_____

_____

_____

_____

_____

_____

_____

_____

Stop protecting your offender with unforgiveness!

Will you forgive your offender/s, by allowing the Lord to work in your life as He is the ultimate forgiver of offenders? (Leave it to God's Judgement)

THE LORD'S PRAYER–Matthew 6:9-13 NIV

This, then, is how you should pray:

"Our Father in heaven,

hallowed be your name,

your kingdom come,

your will be done,

on earth as it is in heaven.

Give us today our daily bread.

And forgive us our debts,

as we also have forgiven our debtors.

And lead us not into temptation,

but deliver us from the evil one."

PSALM 51 (NLT)

For the choir director: A psalm of David, regarding the time Nathan the prophet came to him after David had committed adultery with Bathsheba.

Have mercy on me, O God, because of your unfailing love. Because of your great compassion, blot out the stain of my sins.

Wash me clean from my guilt. Purify me from my sin.

For I recognize my rebellion; it haunts me day and night.

Against you, and you alone, have I sinned; I have done what is evil in your sight. You will be proved right in what you say, and your judgment against me is just.

For I was born a sinner... yes, from the moment my mother conceived me.

But you desire honesty from the womb, teaching me wisdom even there.

Purify me from my sins, and I will be clean; wash me, and I will be whiter than snow.

Oh, give me back my joy again; you have broken me... now let me rejoice.

Don't keep looking at my sins. Remove the stain of my guilt.

Create in me a clean heart, O God. Renew a loyal spirit within me.

Do not banish me from your presence, and don't take your Holy Spirit from me.

Restore to me the joy of your salvation, and make me willing to obey you.

Then I will teach your ways to rebels, and they will return to you.

Forgive me for shedding blood, O God who saves; then I will joyfully sing of your forgiveness.

Unseal my lips, O Lord, that my mouth may praise you.

You do not desire a sacrifice, or I would offer one. You do not want a burnt offering.

The sacrifice you desire is a broken spirit. You will not reject a broken and repentant heart, O God.

Look with favor on Zion and help her; rebuild the walls of Jerusalem.

Then you will be pleased with sacrifices offered in the right spirit, with burnt offerings and whole burnt offerings.

Then bulls will again be sacrificed on your altar.

RESTITUTION

The final step to complete freedom is making sure that you have made your heart right before men as much as possible. Restitution is a biblical principle that explains the issue of dealing aggressively with sin committed towards an individual or organization.

"If anyone sins and commits a breach of faith against the LORD by deceiving his neighbor in a matter of deposit or security, or through robbery, or if he has oppressed his neighbor or has found something lost and lied about it, swearing falsely–in any of all the things that people do and sin thereby–if he has sinned and has realized his guilt and will restore what he took by robbery or what he got by oppression or the deposit that was committed to him or the lost thing that he found or anything about which he has sworn falsely, he shall restore it in full and shall add a fifth to it, and give it to him to whom it belongs on the day he realizes his guilt." Leviticus 6:2-5 ESV

He entered Jericho and was passing through. And there was a man named Zacchaeus. He was a chief tax collector and was rich. And he was seeking to see who Jesus was, but on account of the crowd he could not, because he was small of stature. So he ran on ahead and climbed up into a sycamore tree to see him, for he was about to pass that way. And when Jesus came to the place, he looked up and said to him, "Zacchaeus, hurry and come down, for I must stay at your house today." So he hurried and came down and received him joyfully. And when they saw it, they all grumbled, "He has gone in to be the guest of a man who is a sinner." And Zacchaeus stood and said to the Lord, "Behold, Lord, the half of my goods I give to the poor. And if I have defrauded anyone of anything, I restore it fourfold." Luke 19:1-8 ESV

The Bible is clear that *"if you bring your gift to the altar, and there remember that your brother has something against you, leave your gift there before the altar, and go your way. First be reconciled to your brother, and then come and offer your gift."* Matthew 5:23-24 NKJV

It is important as you go through these steps of forgiveness, that if God highlights to you people whom you may have hurt in past or present relationships, that you go back and 'make things right' through repentance and restoration.

In a case of stealing, whether a small library book to something even larger, it is important to go back to the one it is stolen from in humility and repentance and be willing and ready to pay back for the item stolen. It makes no difference whether the event occurred years prior. God remembers every detail and we should do our best to make our wrongs right.

In the case of a past relationship where the other party may have been wounded by your words or actions, it would also be appropriate to go back and repent to the person for your cruel actions or words. This can be extremely challenging if you have been in multiple relationships and/ or if the person you feel convicted about is no longer in your life. The advice that can be given in these cases is to say "God, I am totally willing and committed, that if you bring the person back in my pathway, to repent and make amends for my sins towards them." But make sure that you mean it because God sometimes will orchestrate those kinds of situations in our lives to ensure we are obedient to what we say.

Why is restitution so important? Because it frees your heart from holding anything hidden in the darkness and it expresses God's heart through your example. It also lets the enemy know that he has no power to hold you in any form of bondage from past 'hidden sins'.

Do not find it unusual if the person you repent to does not accept your apology or agrees with you that you did wrong to them. In these situations, the most important thing is to have an attitude of humility and move on knowing that you are free because you did what was right. Making things right needs to be a constant flow in our hearts because it keeps our spirits sensitive to the Holy Spirit. By blocking out His voice or 'nudging' in our hearts, we are also hindering God from being able to completely flow in and through our lives.

APPLYING RESTITUTION

Take a moment to ask God "Is there anyone from my past or who is currently in my life to whom I need to repent and make amends with?" Write down the names of those He highlights to you in your heart and go and make it right with them. It will not be easy but it is definitely worth your total freedom.

_____

_____

_____

_____

_____

_____

_____

_____

_____

_____

_____

_____

_____

_____

_____

_____

_____

_____

_____

_____

_____

PRAYER OF REPENTANCE

I repent of the sins of my flesh and I am asking you, Lord, to examine my heart, my mind and my emotions. I repent of every sin that I have committed consciously and unconsciously. I ask you Lord to create in me a clean heart and renew your right spirit within me. Please do not cast me away from your presence, and please don't take your Holy Spirit away from me. I repent, Lord, of the sins of anger, bitterness, which have caused unforgiveness in my heart. As I repent Lord, I ask that you would help me to become a living sacrifice unto you, willing to be your servant.

Lord, I ask you to teach me your ways and guide me in your truth. And I will teach others your ways and your truth. I receive your forgiveness in my life now.

In Jesus' name. Amen

PRAYER OF DELIVERANCE

I cover myself with the blood of Jesus and put on the whole armor of God, protecting my mind with the helmet of salvation. I put on the belt of truth, the shield of faith, the sword of the spirit, which is Your Word, the body armor of Your righteousness and for shoes, I put on the peace that comes from the Good News. I come against every fiery dart of the enemy by the power of Jesus' blood.

Lord, I take authority over my thoughts, and command that they will line up with God's truth over my life. I stand against the patterns of fear, doubt, unbelief and command them to flee from my life in Jesus' name. I declare that I am a man/woman of faith, confident hope and belief in Your word.

I command all roots of unforgiveness, anger and bitterness to leave me right now. I command all mental, emotional and physical wounds and torment to flee from my life now in Jesus' name

I renounce all ancestral sins in my life and break off its power over my life. I commit to being a new creation in Christ and declare that I will not live in the sins of my parents or generations prior.

I thank you Lord, that Your promise to me is that goodness and mercy shall follow me all the days of my life and that no weapon that is formed against me will prosper because You have already paid the ultimate price for my sins.

Thank you for this new life of freedom in Jesus' name. Amen.

"O Lord my God, I cried to you for your help, and you restored my health. You brought me up from the grave, O Lord. You kept me from falling into the pit of death." Psalm 30:2-3 NLT

DECLARATION

I declare that from this day forward I will walk in God's complete desire and will for my life which is to live and walk fully free in Him. I declare and decree that who the Son sets free is free indeed. I am the head and not the tail, above and not beneath. I am a royal priesthood, a peculiar person and a chosen generation to declare the praises of God.

I am fearfully and wonderfully made. I declare and decree that God's plans for my life are to prosper and not to harm me. No weapon formed against me shall prosper and every tongue that rises up against me shall be condemned. I am a new creation in Christ. Thank you that Your Word says that you will restore to me the years that the locust has eaten, the cankerworms and the caterpillars and palmerworms (Joel 2:25)

Behold, old things have passed away and now I am made new because of Christ's love and forgiveness in my life.

Thank you Jesus for this new life of freedom.

In Your Powerful Name I pray!

Amen.

SPIKENARD MAGDALENA (OIL)

"There came unto him a woman having an alabaster box of very precious ointment and poured it on his head, as he sat at meat." Matthew 26:7

"And being in Bethany in the house of Simon the leper, as he sat at meat, there came a woman having an alabaster box of ointment of spikenard very precious; and she brake the box, and poured it on his head. And there were some that had indignation within themselves, and said, why was this waste of the ointment made? For it might have been sold for more than three hundred pence, and have been given to the poor. And they murmured against her. And Jesus said, let her alone; why trouble ye her? She hath wrought a good work on me." Mark 14:3-6

"And one of the Pharisees desired him that he would eat with him. And he went into the Pharisee's house, and sat down to meat. And, behold, a woman in the city, which was a sinner, when she knew that Jesus sat at meat in the Pharisee's house, brought an alabaster box of ointment." Luke 7:36-50

Use this well known story in the Bible as a guide to creating your own alabaster box which may include cds, dvds, journals, words of prophecy, testimonies, and whatever the Lord used to minister to you personally. Today is the stepping stone into your destiny which had been delayed by unforgiveness and woundedness!

Remember that according to Revelation 12:11 ESV *"they have conquered him by the blood of the Lamb and by the **word of their testimony...**"*

Thank God that **today** you walk free of ALL unforgiveness, jealousy, bitterness, anger, and every spirit that had attached itself to your heart!

"Is any sick among you? Let him call for the elders of the church and let them pray over him anointing him with oil in the name of the Lord; and the prayer of faith shall save the sick and the Lord shall raise him up, and if he has committed sins, they shall be forgiven, in Jesus name we pray." James 5:14-15

SALVATION PRAYER

Jesus is your FREE PASS to Heaven

"For God so loved the world that He gave His only begotten Son, that whosoever believes in Him will not perish, but have everlasting life."

John 3:16

IF YOU WANT TO BE FREE IN SPIRIT, SOUL & BODY, PRAY
THIS PRAYER...

Dear Lord Jesus, I come to you a sinner. I say today with my mouth and believe in my heart that You died for my sins and were raised from the dead. Come in and take over my life, Jesus. Set my spirit free from sin. Set my soul (mind and emotions) free from torment. Set my body free from all sickness and disease. I receive your complete forgiveness in my life. Fill me with your Holy Spirit. (Romans 10:9-10, Acts 1:8). And I thank you for forgiving and loving me. In Jesus' name I pray. Amen.

Jude 24-25 *"Now to Him who is able keep you from stumbling, And to present you faultless before the presence of His glory with exceeding joy To God our Savior, Who alone is wise, Be glory and majesty, Dominion and power, Both now and forever." Amen*

Forgiveness is the Good News of Jesus Christ.   This is the place to start. FORGIVE!

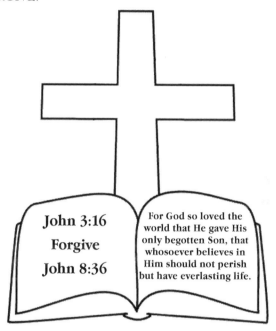

John 3:16

Forgive

John 8:36

For God so loved the world that He gave His only begotten Son, that whosoever believes in Him should not perish but have everlasting life.

ADDITIONAL NOTES:

_____
_____
_____
_____
_____
_____
_____
_____
_____
_____
_____
_____
_____
_____
_____
_____
_____
_____
_____
_____
_____
_____
_____
_____
_____
_____
_____
_____
_____
_____